THE NEW DISSENTERS

The Nonconformist Conscience
in the Age of Thatcher

Walter Schwarz

Bedford Square Press

Published by
BEDFORD SQUARE PRESS of the
National Council for Voluntary Organisations
26 Bedford Square, London WC1B 3HU

First published 1989
Copyright © Walter Schwarz, 1989

Typeset by AKM Associates (UK) Ltd, Southall, London
Printed and bound in England by The Oxford University Press, Oxford

British Library Cataloguing in Publication Data

The new dissenters: the nonconformist
    conscience in the age of Thatcher — (Society Today)
    1. Great Britain. Social conditions
    I. Schwarz, Walter, *1930–*
    II. Series
    941.085'8

ISBN 0-7199-1245-8

S<u>*ociety*</u> **T**<u>*oday*</u>

THE NEW DISSENTERS

The Nonconformist Conscience
in the Age of Thatcher

Walter Schwarz is the *Guardian*'s religious affairs correspondent. He was the paper's correspondent in West Africa in
the sixties, in Israel (1970–2), in India (1972–5) and in France
(1975–84).

He was born in Vienna in 1930 and was educated at Manchester
Grammar School and The Queen's College, Oxford. He is
author of *The Arabs in Israel* (Faber, 1959); *Nigeria* (Pall Mall
Press, 1968); *Breaking Through: The Theory and Practice of
Wholistic Living*, with Dorothy Schwarz (Green Books/
Element Books, 1987); and editor of *Updating God* (Marshall
Pickering, 1988).

He is married, with three daughters and two sons, and lives in
rural Essex.

Contents

In my lifetime the consensus has moved from the right to the centre, to the left, to the hard right. And I suppose you have to cherish Dissenters to every one of them.

Tony Benn, politician

Thatcherism is non-conforming to what most people in Britain believe, except that Thatcher is in government and quite deliberately organising what amounts to a revolution in the British way of life.

Eric Hobsbawm, historian

There's a great common family feeling between inner-city poverty people, Amnesty International people, anti-nuclear people, Green people and the rest . . . There is a different set of values running along in the country, parallel to Thatcher's, which actually hasn't got a voice to express itself at the moment because it doesn't come clearly out of the Labour Party.

Bruce Kent, chairman, CND

If only we could change Britain, bring back the meaning of the whole gospel and take Britain out of institutional and conditional thinking. There was a time in England when people experienced a Reformation, and I believe that history will replay that tape again.

Io Smith, Black Pentecostal leader

Mrs Thatcher keeps on saying that equal rights for women have largely been won, and it may very well be true for a handful of women who have managed to get fairly high up in their own profession. But for the overwhelming mass of women who are amongst the poor, she's not only done nothing: she's made the situation worse.

Jo Richardson, politician

Introduction

Has Mrs Thatcher created a Nonconformist Conscience against her, uniting the churches and high-minded non-believers in a grand moral alliance? It would be an amazing achievement for a Methodist grocer's daughter who promotes, above all else, the virtues of the Protestant ethic. There are solid indications that something of this kind is happening. In moving so radically away from consensus politics, Thatcherism is creating a moral backlash. The Church of England has cast off from its Tory anchorage. Episcopal dissent is mild, or at least mild-mannered, but from the lower ranks of the churches, and even more from believers who are as critical of bishops as of Cabinet ministers, come more robust language. And religious people are not alone in evoking moral, ultimately spiritual values as a counterweight to the official ideology.

These new Nonconformists are everywhere. Some work in voluntary agencies like the Child Poverty Action Group, or hospices, or job schemes run by churches. Others are social workers, teachers or local government officials. Some are on the dole, using their DHSS money for voluntary work.

Many are Christians who do not go to church and are often critical of the church establishments – like the original Nonconformists. Others are socialists, not necessarily in accord with the Labour Party. A growing number consider themselves Conservatives, but are in despair over the Government's deliberate and radical departure from traditional social values.

Some are in the Green movement or the peace movement or, more and more commonly, in both. Some, indeed, combine the lot: Dissenting Christian, Bennite Socialist, CND and Green. Others do without ideology and simply react against, or opt out of, the consumerist free-for-all. What all the protestors have in common is a feeling that Thatcherism has created a new situation calling for a new response.

The new Dissenters are the heirs of the Nonconformist Conscience which contributed in the past to such diverse British achievements as the abolition of slavery and the creation of institutions ranging from trade unions and the Labour Party to the Salvation Army and the *Manchester Guardian*.

It was the *Guardian*'s features editor, Richard Gott, who suggested last year that I might find out what on earth had happened to the Nonconformist Conscience in these dire times. In the enquiry I expected to find myself among musty Methodists, Baptists and Quakers. Instead, I found an embryonic grand alliance of new-style Nonconformists, not all of whom believed in God, and most of whom were not members of an Opposition party.

The original enquiry was published in a series of three *Guardian* articles called 'The New Dissenters'.[1] A few weeks later Mrs Thatcher preached her 'Sermon on the Mound' to a Church of Scotland Assembly in Mound Street, Edinburgh, in which she counter-attacked by defining her own brand of Christian morality. I am not suggesting cause and effect, but the Prime Minister was clearly on the defensive about social morality and was reacting to the very Nonconformism I had featured.

The struggle for the high ground in this area has gone on ever since. Indeed the issue has come to the centre of the stage. As Thatcherism enters a new phase, moving on to the poll tax, the Social Fund and the Education Act, political debate centres increasingly on moral and social values. Mrs Thatcher insists that she is a Christian, while Mr Kinnock likens her to Pontius Pilate washing his hands. When he made that accusation she replied furiously that he was 'debasing everything' by quoting the Bible at Question Time. Some of the new Dissenters are not used to spelling out a moral code and saying what they base it on. Compelled to do so for the first time, they are embarrassed. My original interviewees included the bishops of Durham and Liverpool, the politician Tony Benn, the historian Eric Hobsbawm and the CND leader Bruce Kent, as well as volunteer workers in inner cities and social activists of the churches. I talked to Brian Duckworth of the Methodist Church's Division of Social Responsibility, the Runnymede Trust's Kenneth Leech, the Black Pentecostal leader Io Smith, Usha Prashar of the National Council for Voluntary Organisations, Fran Bennett of the Child Poverty Action Group and many others.

Jonathan Croall, Head of Bedford Square Press, then suggested I expand the material for a book. Before writing it I also interviewed Vernon Bogdanor (on local democracy), Jo Richardson (on the plight of women), Elaine Foster (on black people), Jonathon Porritt (on Green dissent), Tim Brighouse (on education), Hanif Kureishi (on culture) and Richard Kirker (on gay men and lesbians). I was also able to include more extensive quotations from my original interviewees.

Even in this enlarged form, my survey makes no claim to cover the whole ground. It seeks to illustrate disparate aspects of a moral protest that is not yet an alliance but is feeling its way. The Bishop of Durham, David Jenkins, said he was reminded of the situation in the fifteenth century 'before the Reformation, before things coalesced into a new movement, where you've got all sorts of things breaking out everywhere . . . A newness was under the surface and you couldn't tell what was healthy and what was unhealthy.' He asked: 'Can we find a thread of hope and direction to dip into this nearly saturated solution so that positive alternatives . . . can coalesce?' This book assembles some elements of an answer, including those provided by David Jenkins himself.

CHAPTER 1

THE OLD NONCONFORMISTS AND THE NEW

All our political liberties were won in battles for religious liberty, starting with the earliest protests even before the Reformation. And if you look at the trade union movement in the nineteenth century and in parts of Britain today, scratch a shop steward and there's a Methodist lay preacher.

Tony Benn has identified readily with the new Dissenters because he saw himself as the direct heir of the old ones – not just the Quakers and Baptists, but more especially the revolutionary Diggers, Ranters and Levellers of the seventeenth century.

My great-grandfather, Julius Benn, was a Congregationalist minister in East London; William Benn, who must have been a distant ancestor, was ejected for refusing to accept the Act of Uniformity. My mother became the president of the Congregational Federation and my wife comes from a Huguenot family.

He said the Nonconformist connection formed his politics.

The Old Testament, the conflict between the kings and the prophets, the exercise of piety, the preachers of righteousness; it is all very relevant today. The prophetic voice, the people who say that what has to be said, however unpopular it is with those who have power, is absolutely essential.

Benn's argument may have been special pleading, for it justified his political loneliness. Yet he did see himself among the heirs, in a climate of Thatcherite materialism, of the seventeenth-century Quakers, the ardent itinerant Methodists of the eighteenth century (Wesley was a Tory but quite definitely a wet), the pro-Whig, anti-slavery, anti-Corn Law Dissenters of the nineteenth century who founded, among other solid Nonconformist institutions, the *Manchester Guardian*.

In our own century the Nonconformist Conscience was midwife to the labour and trade union movements, and, as Tony Benn insists, Nonconformity in religion was father to democracy.

One of the big differences between the Soviet attitude to the churches and ours is we had a Reformation and they didn't. Their Russian Orthodox Church was the instrument of the Tsar whereas here, having broken the power of the Pope and won the right to worship as we liked, there is a radical church tradition.

I put it to the Russians when I was there and they agreed; it is why they've had all this anti-religious propaganda, whereas the left in Latin America has got its allies among the liberation theologians.

The old Dissenters were Quakers, Baptists, Congregationalists, Unitarians, Methodists or other Free Church. Today the ball has passed to a much wider group. Most of the Church of England has, with varying degrees of commitment, joined the protest; so have the Roman Catholics. The denominations are getting round to praying together and agitating together – a breakthrough for ecumenism that should set official alarm bells ringing. And the modern Dissenters have been joined by secular militants who base their protest on moral criteria.

Eric Hobsbawm, the Marxist historian, pointed out that the original Dissenters had a secular motive for siding with reform: they themselves suffered persecution, or at least discrimination. But he conceded:

The fact that there has been a variety of Protestant sects and groups is fundamental to the development of British political thought. The English Revolution in the seventeenth century, in particular, was virtually made in terms of the vocabulary of religious rebellion and resistance. This makes a substantial difference between countries like Britain and countries in which either Catholicism or Protestantism exist as a monolithic state religion – Lutheranism in many parts of Germany or for that matter Calvinism in the Church of Scotland. Breakaways in these countries were possible, but did not have much political spin-off.

Hobsbawm added that the way in which nineteenth-century religious Dissenters organised themselves became a model later for the organisation of secular forms of dissent.

Religious Nonconformity is older by a century than the Reformation. In the fourteenth century John Wycliffe, appealing directly to the Scriptures, inspired the translation of the Bible into English and the Lollards in their revolt. Congregationalists worshipped at secret meetings in defiance of Elizabeth's Act of Uniformity in the sixteenth century and, a century later, most of the pilgrim fathers sailing to America in the *Mayflower* were Separatists and Puritans. Already, Quakers, Unitarians and Baptists were providing the recruits for political radicalism. These were the Levellers and Diggers whom Tony Benn identifies with. Nonconformity had taken root and the Restoration could not uproot it: the 1662 Act of Uniformity established it permanently on the scene.

Wesleyan Methodism was mainly concerned with spiritual renewal, and in the eighteenth century there was never any intention to break away from the Church of England. However, the Nonconformist evangelism of the eighteenth century was never far removed from political dissent, and that link was greatly strengthened in the nineteenth century. Dissent was to play a prominent role in the Anti-Corn Law League, the Ten Hours Act which established a ten-hour working day, agitation for state education and Chartism – all of which were strands which produced the Liberal Party.

The nineteenth-century Nonconformists had a *laissez-faire* attitude to the state, restricting government activities. Methodists such as Wilberforce, Shaftesbury, Bright and Cobden thought society should be reformist. It was all very middle class, but political Nonconformity became the ally of working-class discontent, in a common attack on the entrenched positions of the Establishment, both political and religious. By the end of the century that common interest was gone; as the disabilities waned, so dissent gave way to smug conformism.

The historian Adrian Hastings describes the Nonconformist world at the turn of the century as follows:

It existed on the interface of skilled artisan and petty industrialist, self contained and self assured, intensely local: glorying in honest work, pietistic in speech, unhesitatingly intolerant in its insistence upon conformity to the norms of Nonconformity. Methodism begins as high Tory, but also came to be against squire and parson and large parish church in town.[1]

William Booth, founder of the Salvation Army, was a former Methodist minister. George Cadbury, in the family tradition, founded his Birmingham chocolate factory based on the motto: 'The service of God is the service of man.' Later, middle-class Nonconformity turned Conservative while working-class Nonconformity turned to the Labour Party. Hastings traces the story through to Thatcherite times.

The consensus which had effectively ruled Britain in the days of Stanley Baldwin, Ramsay MacDonald and Neville Chamberlain, which had found its major prophets in Tawney, Beveridge and Temple, its achievers in Attlee, Cripps, Macmillan and Butler, was no more.[2]

Munsey Turner, a modern historian of Methodism, recalled that Nonconformity declined after the great Liberal landslide of 1906: 'Christianity as a whole weakened its hold and the Nonconformist view became irrelevant. A long line of lapsed

Dissenters has stretched from Ernest Bevin and Neville Chamberlain to Margaret Thatcher and including Michael Foot and Harold Wilson.'

Today Methodists are very conscious of being overtaken in their dissent. Their grandest old man, Lord Soper, who has been preaching on Tower Hill every Wednesday since 1926, said he saw Methodism as 'the preaching order within the holy Catholic church rather than as a denomination set against others', and that he

> cannot see in the future the perpetuation of a denomination such as the Methodist Church but there's a real need of the kind of preaching order John Wesley helped to create. I follow in the steps of John Wesley. Though he was a High Tory, he took the message outside and I believe that it's even more important now because probably Hyde Park or Tower Hill are two of the remaining unfettered occasions.

Are Methodists still in the frontline? Brian Duckworth, general secretary of their Division of Social Responsibility, thought that the area of confrontation had changed in the last 50 years: 'Then, it was between the haves and have-nots. Now it's between those who operate within a kingdom-centred theology and those who take the world as it is, content with second best. Dissenters wrestle with possibilities that others call utopian.' Duckworth said that the appeal of Wesleyanism used to be to people with a social conscience – people who imagined they could have the Kingdom of Heaven on earth.

> We had the Webbs, Fabians, trade unions, friendly societies, the co-operative movement, Quakers, sons and daughters of the Free Church manse. Butskellism was the golden era of their fruits. But in the last 40 years there's been the difficulty of funding all this. The 'kingdom' has proved financially unviable.

He pointed to the following two aspects of the Nonconformist experience.

First, respect for hard work, maximising your talents, a routine which Wesley deplored not for itself, but for its consequences. He all but lamented: 'I've turned them into yuppies.' Second, identification with the underdog and redistributive justice. Mrs Thatcher thought that in the 'broader pastures' of C. of E. (where she went from her native Methodism) she could leave the second aspect behind. But the Anglicans are now just as concerned about disparities of wealth as the Nonconformists.

Today there is a new Nonconformity which has almost given up on political protest in despair, and gone off into self-selecting 'networks and communities'. This despair in the political process is a new development. We mustn't abandon the political process: we must train young people to engage politically. Many issues we had thought resolved – such as the role of government in effecting redistributive justice on behalf of society – have to be brought back to the centre again.

The new Methodists are predominantly bourgeois. Brian Beck, Secretary of their Conference, said that the Roman Catholics were now much more working class.

Free churches are the lower middle class rather than labouring classes. The Salvation Army and the Romans manage to be both, while Methodism isn't a distinct social category. Some Thatcherite values get through to us. Among our ministers a very strong proportion read the *Guardian*; in the pews, judging by the letters I get, they read the *Daily Telegraph*, the *Daily Express* and *Daily Mail*. And yet all Methodists retain a tradition of social concern and that modifies the danger of Thatcherism.

Munsey Turner thought that Methodism still represented freedom from links with the state,

. . . though the Church of England is not all that linked to the state now. The big change is that Roman Catholics are now

part of English dissent. They're the strongest force,
particularly on the moral side. They've taken over the role
that free churches had at the end of the nineteenth century;
they prod on moral issues, especially personal morality –
abortion most of all.

The Quakers are still intensely interested in dissent, especially
Green ideas and the peace movement. Their tradition of big-
business charity also remains unbroken. Donald Southall, who
runs the Quakers' London headquarters, said his father had
done a family tree which showed nearly 100 families, almost all
in the Quaker tradition. He pointed out that 'Many of the
present charitable trusts have strong Quaker roots, such as the
Joseph Rowntree Charitable Trust and the Barrow and
Geraldine Cadbury Trust: the Cadbury Trust includes a
particular focus on local needs in cities, Rowntree on peace
initiatives and research on sources of conflict.'

The Quakers have spent years looking for ways to divert to
non-military use that portion of their income tax which they
believe is being used for armaments. As Southall explained:

Some of the past Quakers went to prison for refusing
military service, and today conscientious objection is very
widely recognised. We cannot willingly fuel the fire through
our taxes. One of our Yearly Meeting sessions was devoted
to the issue. Some members are witholding what they think is
the right proportion of their taxes and seek to divert the
money to a fund for peaceful purposes. They say they'll pay
when the Government tells them where to send it. Others
send cheques to various funds. But if they're sent to the tax
office they bank them no matter what's written on the
cheque.

For two years the Society witheld a portion of PAYE payments
for some of its staff, telling the Inland Revenue that the money
would be available for a useful fund. It went through the courts
and appeal, to the House of Lords. In each case the Government won. The Society released the money and took the case to

the European Court of Appeal which refused on a technicality to look at it. Southall said that they would 'go on until we get something: we have a committee working on it right now'.

The landscape of dissent has changed: the actors, the causes of action and the targets are different. But the spirit of morally based disagreement remains, and there are signs of a new flowering.

CHAPTER 2

THATCHERISM IS IMMORAL

Morality has moved to the centre of the debate. It was not always so. In the days known as Thatcherism Mark One, economics and labour practices held centre-stage. Moral issues were skirted, often wrapped in vague references to neo-Victorian values, with strong echoes of the Protestant work ethic. But there was always a Thatcherite morality underneath. It was privileged information, uttered inside quasi-academic institutions and available in the obscure textbooks of the New Right. No doubt it was considered unnecessary, even dangerous, to flaunt the hidden moral agenda.

Later, as the prevailing policies began to 'bite', as a new underclass of victims of Thatcherite policies began to emerge, as inner cities decayed and public services available to the poor declined, the moral debate became unavoidable.

By subtle stages, the Church of England moved into opposition. It ceased to be the Tory Party at prayer. Rumblings of episcopal discontent were followed by the Archbishop of Canterbury's Falklands sermon, in which he infuriated the triumphant war leader by failing to sound triumphant. Then came the Archbishop's *Faith in the City* report in 1985, denounced as 'Marxist' by a Cabinet minister even before it was published. It was the church's first systematic attempt at questioning Thatcherite values. The Church of England found itself at the centre of an embryonic moral alliance, not with the political Opposition but with other churches, individual Dissenters and scores of voluntary bodies such as the Child Poverty Action Group.

These and other attacks eventually put the Government on the defensive. The reaction was Mrs Thatcher's elaborate 'Sermon on the Mound', preached on 21 May 1988 to a Church of Scotland Assembly in Mound Street, Edinburgh. Mrs Thatcher had at last enunciated her religion. The 'Sermon' provoked an immediate counter-attack, for it had been a lame, disingenuous and starkly one-sided interpretation of the gospels. As a result, the 1988 Tory Party Conference focused once again on the social morality of Government policies.

The Labour Party might have provided the rallying point for this moral opposition. Some of its leaders seized the debating opportunity, but the party as a whole did not rise to the occasion. It was preoccupied with internal struggles; it needed to appeal to the electorate in an increasingly consumerist atmosphere; and its thinking was too rigidly secular to find a convincing moral formulation. So the churches took a lead.

Churches should be 'both locally and more broadly a centre of resistance'. The proposition comes not from a hotheaded Christian radical but from David Sheppard, the Anglican partner in Liverpool's unusual episcopal double act – the other half being his Roman Catholic friend, Derek Worlock.

Being a centre of resistance doesn't mean we've got to lay down the law. A new curate was elected chairman of his local community council: more experienced clergy persuaded him that wasn't quite his role. The church works out its servant role when we respect and support local leadership. Many are glad to see the church involved in the life of the whole community. They have longed to see that the church was alive in the way they think Jesus would be, and feel we often haven't been.

In the book he wrote with Worlock, Sheppard says that living in Canning Town and Woolwich changed his mind about the gospel.

It would not be too much to say I experienced another conversion – conversion to Christ in the city. When I was

ordained, I believed that the gospel was about changing
individuals and gradually we would change the world. I still
believe it is about changing people from inside out, but I
came to see that we are also called to change the course of
events, as far as that lies within our power.[1]

A vicar in Liverpool's volatile Toxteth district, Simon
Starkey, thought that the David and Derek act has had a
'dramatic effect' in getting like-minded people of all faiths, and
none, together. 'I think of it as community theology; it's not
necessarily religious,' he said. 'There's a political void, not a
moral one. A void that friendly, astute and relevant clergy get
into. Politicians, national or local, don't rate at all in Toxteth;
the clergy do.'

Starkey is chairman of the local hostel for black teenagers
and an official of a housing association. He was instrumental in
setting up a community work project (paid for by the Church
of England's Children's Society) to help people cope with a
variety of problems. In his work he finds 'more and more
people actually coping – they're in touch with each other,
learning how to cope with shortage through self-help groups.
And there's this new ecumenical thing, so you actually talk to
someone who goes to a Catholic church.' He has also noticed
that 'many of our customers don't come to church but most of
them pray'.

In a different sector of the turbulent bishops' front line,
David Jenkins, Bishop of Durham, reacted sorrowfully to the
Government's current attempt to enlist the church for spread-
ing moral values as an antidote to crime. That, he said, is how
Marx and the sociologist Durkheim interpreted religion – as
'social bonding'.

To accept that is simply to sell the pass; it's to say these
criticisms of religion are right: religion is simply something
to do with the bonding of society and with the projective
needs of individuals. That may be how God gets into our
consciousness; that may be an important way of understanding religion, pilgrimage and spirituality.

But God is far, far more than that: he is himself or herself a disturber; and you might even say he's a great Nonconformist. Where does the biblical tradition start? With God disturbing Abraham. Where does the Exodus start? With God disturbing Moses. And what happens when Jesus comes is so deeply disturbing that he is crucified and, what is more, crucified by a combination of the religious and civil authorities.

We have to be reminded of all this by prophetic movements (with a small 'p') within the churches and outside; groups of persons who recover this sense of refusing to put up with all the denials and all the tamings and all the conformings.

Dr Jenkins interpreted the row in the Church of England over the controversial preface to *Crockford's Directory* for 1988, which criticised the liberal leadership of the church, as 'a reminder that, as the Bible shows, this is an endemic struggle, always will be until the end. The church has always to be reformed. There is always the conforming to an inadequate or insufficient form, whether it is society or the church.'

One of the great sources of disaster in Eastern European societies is that the Marxist ultra-utopians thought the kingdom had arrived, and you had to be conformed to society as worked out by Lenin and taken over by Stalin. Mercifully you get Nonconformists, though they may have to go to the gulag. Wherever you are, I would say this business of Nonconformity and Dissenting is a very important response to the continuing, struggling spirit of God.

The Church of England and the Roman Catholics are, of course, joined by the Nonconformist churches in the protest. The Methodist Church's Division of Social Responsibility denounced the Government's social policies in March 1988, saying that the proposed community charge, or poll tax, 'compounds injustice with complexity'. The Division said that it was deeply concerned by proposals which 'impose new and excessive burdens on the poor' and were not acceptable 'to the individual Christian conscience'.

The churches' response to the effects of Thatcherism in the cities covered a wide ideological spectrum, ranging from the sadly constructive to angry rejection. *Faith in the City* (1985) put a stern question mark on the Government's priorities.

The creation of wealth must go hand in hand with just distribution . . . There is a long Christian tradition reaching back into the Old Testament prophets, and supported by influential schools of economic and political thought, which firmly rejects the amassing of wealth unless it is justly obtained and fairly distributed. If these provisos are not insisted upon, the creation of wealth cannot go unchallenged as a first priority of national policy.

The debate has moved on since 1985. The Reverend John Austin, writing in the summer 1988 issue of the Child Poverty Action Group's journal *Poverty*, took a more radical view.

Faith in the City, published in 1985, has guided and informed much of the churches' response to this government in the field of social policy. Its position of critical and, hopefully, creative solidarity, is based on the premise that it is preferable to work *with* the government for the good of the people, than in *opposition* to it. Its basic assumptions were of consensus politics; in other words, the report assumed the churches and the government to have the same ultimate aims and objectives – of working for justice and the improved wellbeing of all the people. This in turn assumed that it was enough for good men and women to describe what was happening for certain sections of the community for policies to change. The report failed completely to perceive that a very different body of people were in the driving seat of government and were guided by attitudes and assumptions very different from its own.

Austin concludes, in common with an increasing number of

Christian commentators, that 'the elevation of individual freedom and choice as the goal of social policy is at total variance with the Christian tradition'.

In the early part of 1988, moral indignation against Thatcherism moved into a still higher gear. The Home Secretary, Douglas Hurd, had tried to enlist support from the Church of England's General Synod in fighting crime by getting the church to 'do its job' of instilling Christian values. Dr Runcie's reaction was polite – too polite for more radical church critics. Kenneth Leech, director of the Runnymede Trust, wrote in the *Guardian*'s 'Face to Faith' column.[2]

On the one hand, we have a government whose leaders seem to be effectively ignorant of the entire tradition of Christian social thought and action (an ignorance for which they are not for the most part to blame, for the tradition itself has been in decay for some time) and whose view of what constitutes the essence of Christianity does not coincide with the theology or spirituality of any mainstream Christian church. On the other, we have a church which is so lacking in confidence that it has to defend, in the most genteel and apologetic way, positions which are so moderate and reformist that they would have caused not a flicker in a less reactionary period. Yet because the government has moved so far to the right, the church, by staying in the same place, looks more radical than it is. In the present climate, one does not need to do very much to be seen as leftwing, Marxist or 'trendy'.

Leech argued that both the Thatcher and the Reagan governments were at almost every point in conflict with biblical teaching and with traditional Christian principles:

. . . the nuclear commitment, the neglect of the alien, the orphan and the widow, the oppression of the poor, the maintenance and extension of inequality, the encouragement of selfishness and greed, the creation of a climate in which

racism, bigotry and intolerance can flourish more than at
any point in recent years – all these things are done in the
name of the 'moral order'. The church has been slow to
resist, and it is cause for rejoicing that there is some evidence
of a movement of Christian resistance. But at the level of the
established church, it is all so proper, so refined, so lacking in
zeal and passion and theological critique. The sun has gone
down on the prophets with a vengeance. All that remains is
reformist tinkering.

The church needs to go on the offensive. It has nothing to
lose but its chains. Established or not, allied with Mammon
or not, it can begin to disentangle itself, to disaffiliate from
the Mammon-worshipping order. In fact it does so whenever
it celebrates the Eucharist, though most of those who assist
at Holy Communion would be reluctant to be termed Holy
Communists. But what is needed is for that resistance to be
made explicit and to be organised. In the cruel climate of
Reagan–Thatcherdom those who stand for justice and for
the defence of the poor, whether they are Christian or not,
are understandably concerned to keep warm and to nourish
one another. When the days are evil, the natural tendency is
to put survival first. But it is not enough to keep warm:
rigorous critique, the proclamation of the gospel of the
kingdom, the return to the prophetic word, are needed.

Mrs Thatcher's calculated counter-attack against her moral
critics was made in her address to the Church of Scotland's
General Assembly in Edinburgh in May 1988. 'Speaking
personally as a Christian, as well as a politician, about the way
I see things', she quoted with approval the dictum that
'Christianity is about spiritual redemption, not social reform.'
She continued:

Sometimes the debate on these matters has become too
polarised and given the impression that the two are quite
separate. Most Christians would regard it as their personal
Christian duty to help their fellow men and women ... These
duties come not from any secular legislation passed by

Parliament, but from being a Christian ... What then are the distinctive marks of Christianity? They stem not from the social but from the spiritual side of our lives.

She identified three beliefs in particular:

First, that from the beginning, man has been endowed by God with the fundamental right to choose between good and evil. Second, that we were made in God's own image and therefore we are expected to use all our own power of thought and judgement in exercising that choice; and further, if we open our hearts to God, he has promised to work within us. And third, that Our Lord Jesus Christ, the Son of God, when faced with his terrible choice and lonely vigil, chose to lay down his life that our sins may be forgiven.

Mrs Thatcher quoted St Paul's words 'if a man will not work he shall not eat', in support of her thesis that all must work to create wealth. Abundance, she argued, had a 'legitimacy which derives from the very nature of Creation'. However, she did acknowledge that there were limits.

The Tenth Commandment – Thou shalt not covet – recognises that making money and owning things could become selfish activities. But it is not the creation of wealth that is wrong, but love of money for its own sake. The spiritual dimension comes in deciding what one does with the wealth. How could we respond to the many calls for help, or invest for the future, or support the wonderful artists and craftsmen whose work also glorifies God, unless we had first worked hard and used our talents to create the necessary wealth?

This was the germ of her new theme of 'active citizenship' which she was to develop at the 1988 Party Conference.

Any set of social and economic arrangements which is not founded on the acceptance of individual responsibility will do nothing but harm. We are all responsible for our own actions. We cannot blame society if we disobey the law. We simply cannot delegate the exercise of mercy and generosity to others.

The politicians and other secular powers . . . can only see that the laws encourage the best instincts and convictions of the people, instincts and convictions which I am convinced are far more deeply rooted than is often supposed. Nowhere is this more evident than the basic ties of the family which are at the heart of our society and are the very nursery of civic virtue. It is on the family that we in government build our own policies for welfare, education and care.

The 'Sermon on the Mound' was demolished in detail and at leisure by more orthodox moralists. 'Can we understand personal responsibility without stressing also the essentially social character of human life?' asked the Bishop of Gloucester in a letter to Mrs Thatcher. His own answer was 'the social character is fundamental and inescapable'.

Dr Mark Corner, lecturer in religious studies at the University of Newcastle upon Tyne, wrote in the *Guardian*'s 'Face to Faith' column [3] suggesting that Mrs Thatcher might

. . . turn for a moment from those pious platitudes about individual giving which she culls from a handful of New Testament texts to the prophetic Old Testament denunciation of nations and cities in which the poor went uncared for and the rich enjoyed their wealth. The prophets could tell her something about the progressive decline of a nation as the fat cats get fatter, as the manners and attitudes of the people grow uglier and as the poorest minority is swept out of sight. And they could tell her that change can realistically come, not when the rich turn from their wealth to help the poor, but when the nation expresses its commitment to the morality of public provision by taking away some of their wealth.

Returning to her new theme in a later speech, Mrs Thatcher quoted with approval Wesley's exhortation to 'gain all you

can, save all you can, give all you can'. Refuting that, Brian
Duckworth, general secretary of the Methodist Church's
Division of Social Responsibility, accused her of misinter-
preting Wesley's words. Far from supporting Thatcherism,
Wesley would have been 'shocked' at much of the Government's recent legislation – particularly the 1988 Budget and the
social security changes. Duckworth pointed out that Wesley
might have intended his sermon as a counter-attack on Adam
Smith's *The Wealth of Nations*, that most-respected source of
modern Tory economic thought. Duckworth went on:

> Wesley was shocked by the contrast between the newly rich
> and the grinding misery of the poor . . . The public might
> think that by quoting 'give all you can', it's what's left over
> that's to be used among the poor, but that's not the case.
> Wesley meant 'give until it hurts'. It's not a sermon about
> motivation, but about giving all you can and making that a
> priority. A lot of people would think that by quoting the
> phrase 'gain all you can', the current free market approach
> to the economy was legitimate as far as Wesley was
> concerned. Whereas, of course, he would not think that . . .
> Wesley would have been shocked at the recent Budget. He
> would have been shocked at the recent changes in the social
> security legislation in that they have made the poor even
> poorer . . . He would have been shocked by the contrast of
> extreme wealth and extreme poverty. He would want human
> need met in organised ways. He did not wish it done only
> through philanthropy.

At the end of 1988, the battle for the high moral ground
continued to rage. In September Mrs Thatcher surprised the
media with a concerned speech about ecological problems, and
the following month the Conservative Party Conference put
'citizenship' on its agenda. The Prime Minister hinted at a new
philosophy in which concern for the needy was expressed in
individual charity rather than community action. She said that
personal effort did not undermine the community, but
enhanced it.

There will always be a minority whose sole concern is themselves. But those who care, and they are the great majority of us, now have the means to give. The fact is that prosperity has created not the selfish society but the generous society . . . Does someone's natural desire to do well for himself, to build a better life for his family and provide opportunities for his children . . . make him a materialist? Of course it doesn't . . . the truth is that what we are actually encouraging is the best in human nature.

On the other side, moral critics continued to lament the lack of a credible political alternative. Some Dissenters switched their attack to the church establishment, demanding a new Reformation. Others, as we see in the next chapter, expressed their protest in action, working to help the disadvantaged in decayed inner cities.

CHAPTER 3

DISSENT FROM BELOW

The Unofficial Church

Like the original Nonconformists, many of the new Dissenters are as much in arms against their own church as against the enactments of the Thatcherite state. They are looking for a new Reformation.

Kenneth Leech, a prominent guru of angry Christians, founder of the left-wing Anglo-Catholic Jubilee Group and director of the anti-racist Runnymede Trust, said that he found Christian radicals 'increasingly on the edge of all the churches. The real divide among Christians now cuts across the historic Reformational ones – between those who believe that the good news of the Kingdom of God involves the transformation of this world and those who don't.' In this new division, Leech felt that the old Nonconformist Conscience was barely relevant, and that Anglo-Catholicism was perhaps even less so.

> I'm an 'Anglo-Catholic' myself, in the sense that that is my theological perspective. But it's an exhausted religious movement; it has fulfilled its role. The good things have been taken on board by the Second Vatican Council, the Liberation theologians and evangelical radicals.

Looking back to traditional Nonconformism, Leech drew a distinction between religious and secular strands.

> The key thing in its growth was the doctrine of holiness, and

the way in which Wesley's emphasis on holiness led to a stress on perfection, originally in personal terms, later in social terms. It led to the anti-slavery movement in America, but in this country it wasn't quite such a close connection: the opposition to slavery came from other sources. Today very few people in the Labour Party are traditional Nonconformist Conscience. Tony Benn was influenced by the Levellers and the Diggers and the John Ball tradition: he's a sort of on-the-fringe Nonconformist. Eric Heffer is an Anglo-Catholic: no Nonconformist Conscience there at all. The vast majority of Labour MPs have not come from that tradition which has been in decline. It was very powerful in the twenties and thirties up to the Second World War. Harold Wilson is almost the last fling – a Methodist local preacher. It's quite important still among older Methodists – that tradition of spirituality and social justice combined.

As a student, Leech was influenced by Stanley Evans, parish priest in East London, later Chancellor of Southwark Cathedral, who began the notion of non-residential training for the Ministry.

In the mid-fifties Stanley's theme was that the real divide among Christians in the future would cut across the historic Reformational ones, and it would divide basically about the understanding of the Kingdom of God. This would cut right across Roman Catholics, Anglicans, Methodists and the rest. You find this divide in Methodism: the Association of Radical Methodists against the others. And among Catholics too; take Chicago, where South-side Jesuits can't be put on the North side. And the Southern Baptists, the most reactionary denomination in the USA and the biggest church; but if you go to their seminary in Louisville, you find the devotees of Thomas Merton and Martin Luther King.

Leech does not rate Anglican bishops highly for their social commitment, in spite of their new-found social indignation.

The church isn't radical even by the standards of the 1930s. When you compare Runcie with Temple or Gore or Blunt, or compare *Faith in the City* with the report of the Archbishop's Commission in 1919, the modern reports appear very restrained. Or even the Lambeth Conference of 1880. You don't have to do much today to be labelled radical left wing or Marxist, you only have to breathe. Most of the bishops could happily go back to the days of Edward Heath, a good Tory Anglican gentleman, and not this grocer's daughter who doesn't understand the church. Heath was compassionate but didn't want to change the capitalist structure any more than the bishops do. Instead they got this woman, an upstart as far as they're concerned; they're mostly public school/Oxbridge. They haven't moved, it's the Government that has moved so far to the right.

The Roman Catholic Bruce Kent, the peace movement leader, stands in the same tradition as Leech. He hardly goes through a day in the chairman's office at CND without experiencing the new dissent as wider than the peace movement.

There's a great common family feeling between inner-city poverty people, Amnesty International people, anti-nuclear people, Green people, and the rest. It's quite hard maintaining CND as a single-issue campaign: I'm asked to go on an Aids march, a housing march, an anti-Apartheid march and so on. I can't do them all. There is a different set of values running along in the country, parallel to Thatcher's, which actually hasn't got a voice to express itself at the moment because it doesn't come clearly out of the Labour Party. There are individuals in the Labour Party but the party looks and behaves as a monolithic structure like the others; salaries are in pyramid and so on. It should campaign for proportional representation which is manifestly just, but doesn't for its own interest. I have recently joined the party – you go in *faute de mieux*; how else can you oppose Thatcher?

His complaint against Rome is the absence of moral leadership in vital areas.

What comes out of Rome is Western – an emphasis on religious rights, a priority on our sufferings as religious people; not on the fact that one person in three who starves to death in the world today is a child under six: that is the real human-rights outrage of the world. The best and most radical thing the Pope did was an address to the Pontifical Academy about three years ago saying that scientists should refuse to work on weapons of mass destruction.

Rome should be internationalist and independent; it could take a leaf out of the Quaker book: Quakers support all kinds of peace-making institutions and proposals. It could support serious funding of the campaign against the arms trade; the churches could sponsor visits and studies about the Soviet Union and socialist countries, do something about the image of the enemy. The Pope believes Russian communism is the enemy; he has two standards on political involvement, one for Nicaragua and one for Poland.

Kent is constantly on the look-out for a Christian community in his locality where issues of justice and peace are discussed and acted on.

I'm trying to form a group where we can meet once a week, not élitist, not splitting off from the parish, meeting before or after the Sunday service to look at the gospel and actually think about social action. People feel Sunday worship is not feeding their spiritual life. I like the Methodists' delegation of authority, I like the Quakers' silence. But they're rather middle class and respectable; only in a Catholic church do I find that I can mix with people who've just come off digging rails up at Euston station.

Our own bishops are mobilised into highly sophisticated political action over the Abortion Bill – yet over six years they had nothing clear to say about cruise missiles or Trident submarines. We have an infinite number of bishops who will support any kind of middle-range option, a freeze or a test ban, but they will not come out to say: this nuclear race is immoral and that there is no justification for Britain having a nuclear weapon. While they stand away from this central issue they hand it to the Tories because they're not campaigning on the issue which has political reality. The church could have been so different, that's what's so heartbreaking. For the 1980 Liverpool Congress the hierarchy produced a marvellous document; it was a moment when people like me felt the Second Vatican Council was actually going to operate in this country. But it was all put on the back burner; within a year it was finished.

Cardinal Hume has said that nuclear arms are only acceptable in the short run, yet the hierarchy has not supported any moves on disarmament. The Pope suppressed his own Star Wars report and did nothing to support the Soviet 18-month nuclear test ban; everything he has done accepts the Western political perspective.

Kent's complaint is shared by younger Catholics all over the country. Liam Black, a layman who co-ordinates the Liverpool Archdiocese Justice and Peace group, thinks Rome and the bishops should be as intransigent on the nuclear issue as they are on abortion. He blames this attitude on the structure of the church.

The Catholic Church looks like the established church and the C. of E. makes the running. The anti-abortion fight motivated us for life unborn, but what about when it's born; pro-life has to be from womb to tomb. The diocese meets monthly; we talk a lot about parishes but I've yet to come across a parish community. Like Brazil we have to break down into smaller communities. The groundwork is being done but it's a long way away.

When asked what Roman Catholic Dissenters could do to resist both Thatcherism and the shortcomings of their church, Black answered: 'Lifestyle is the thing now, the way you actually live.'

What the gospel has to offer as opposed to the Labour Party

is that it's a world that challenges us as individuals at our very roots, our relationships with other people as well as political options. My own lifestyle is one of contradiction and excessive consumption: you can't change that on your own; it has to be a complete family at least.

I was a teacher and involved in resistance. I'd read of the Catholic Worker movement in the USA and the Sojourners' Community. I used to think it was all about issues but I think it's more about trying to develop within the church communities of people that have deep roots and can live out the Thatcher years. The Labour Party is not a potent force to stand against the wind of change that seems to be around, that there's no such thing as society, that it's all individuals – get on by yourself; don't worry about the poor. We've got to develop within the church these communities of resistance, whether they're small Justice and Peace groups, or peace movement or youth groups, they must have a scriptural base but develop the skills of social analysis so that resistance will be deep-rooted and won't just be blown away as so many political organisations have. Also, getting people involved in campaigns on individual issues. This is stuff the third world has developed before us; we have learned from them.

In Liverpool the spirit of dissent has penetrated the Catholic priesthood – and the target is church as well as state. Monsignor Jim Dunne, parish priest and secretary to the Liverpool Archbishop's Council, said: 'Where do we look for constructive dissent? On the whole not in the church.'

A minority in each of the Christian denominations are possessed of this sense of injustice. They feel that to be Christian you have to do something about it; I suspect it's a tiny minority. Maybe we've always been talking about a fraction of church people inspired by their faith to have been at the forefront of change. The interpretation of Christianity has been subtly twisted by the vast majority in a very human way; they've rationalised the gospel to fit a comfortable way of life, as in South Africa today and the southern USA during slavery.

Austin Smith, a Passionist priest who is on the management committees of the Law Centre for the underprivileged and of the Black Technology Centre in Liverpool, complained of the 'gentrification of Christ through the centuries'. He explained that

> It was in the Catholic movements, sects and orders that you had a search for the stark reality of Christ, the naked Christ. I wouldn't want anything simple today but that was very real. We must change the symbolism of religious life, moving closer to where people are. The identification of the office of bishop with almost a worldly structure of career and power is the wrong symbolism. Politically, too, there's room to apply that same formula.

Austin Smith's brand of dissent is monastic, in the spirit of the Franciscans.

> Passionists are people who go round giving mission in various parishes. At first I regarded this urban mission as an extension of what my order has always been: but when I came here I found the horror of 'inner-cityism', which demanded a re-think of what the church is. I'm not in opposition but am disturbed by the way the church leaves the powerlessness of the people as an issue to be addressed rather than a reality to be changed.

He advocates a 'theologising ministry', of small groups, away from large congregations, in which prayer and social conscious-ness would be linked.

> You must have a church that in its ministry is witnessing to a certain sense of powerlessness and humility. Our archbishop and the bishops are extremely dedicated but in the pyramid organisation of society they can't be anything other than

what they are. I don't believe one is going to change this vast church. Religious orders tend to start with protest spirituality and then get sucked into the wider church.

Inside the Cities

'Places to me speak louder than words,' said Jane Galbraith, who lives in a tower block in Camberwell where people urinate in the lift shaft and graffiti cover the corridors. 'Living here helps to understand some of the tensions,' she said. 'I wouldn't feel right coming in from a better area and working with the people as an outsider; I wouldn't have that feeling of belonging and would not have an awful lot of energy and enthusiasm.'

Jane is in her late twenties. She job-shares three days a week, looking after people who are alone for various reasons – because they are new in the area, or are single mothers, because they are black in a white area, made redundant at 50, or have been in mental hospitals. Living by choice near her work makes Jane an 'incomer' in the jargon of Christian social workers. She is a successor, in Thatcher's Britain, of those high-minded Christians and socialists who 'slummed it' in urban 'settlements' in the fifties and sixties. 'Today such incomers tend to be liberal or radical, and have positive feelings about living in a multi-cultural neighbourhood', says a study on Christianity in the inner city. 'They tend to be into things like wholefood, CND, anti-apartheid and cycling and are keen to be involved in the community.' Jane did not say if she was into all those things, or not. She graduated in science and went on to do voluntary work.

> There are five of us in the block. We visit each other, sometimes talk of moving out, we don't know how long we will do it. I think biblically that the point is to be in the community. My background is Anglican but they placed me at this Baptist church in Camberwell. I was working in housing, youth work and visiting, and I got hooked. I've become a Baptist. For an adult believer Baptism is a sign of

profession of faith as an adult: your personal relationship with God rather than promises made on your behalf as a child by other adults.

She works at a settlement in Bermondsey run by the Bede Association, formed 50 years ago when people moved into the inner city to do 'good works'. Jane and her friends do not feel that they form a movement. They translate dissent into a lifestyle. These new Nonconformists provide an ironic answer to the Government's current reproach that the churches have become too political and are not doing enough to re-moralise Britain and thereby help to fight crime. Jane Galbraith said:

About Mrs Thatcher, one of the things that really hurts is that she says people should be standing on their own two feet. I just find that for me that's not possible: I actually need other people. I think the present policies have alienated those who are already the most powerless. In Bermondsey there are people doing OK out of the new dockland, able to buy a house and make money on it; it's the others who have no choice in housing. The decent council houses have been sold off; they're in temporary accommodation that's going to remain temporary for the next ten years of their lives, because there's nothing else. They are struggling to survive, let alone be politicised. Among them there are people who are strong and with encouragement will come out as leaders of the community.

The inner-city Dissenters feel that Thatcherism has created a new situation calling for a new response. Roger Dowley, who also lives in Camberwell, and a veteran among Christian 'incomers' into the city, said he had never been 'a strong party-political person'.

But Mrs Thatcher has done more to make me political than anything in my life: the way she's dismantled so much good, pushing us back to pre-Dickens pauperism; the terminology she uses. Her predecessors did speak as though they cared. She doesn't even bother to appear to be caring.

Dowley is a fourth-generation family solicitor, and fifth-generation Baptist.

I'm just a conventional Baptist. When I made my Christian profession at the age of 17 in 1932 I got bitten with the idea that it wasn't a valid presentation of the Christian faith if the poor and the oppressed were not represented at least 50 per cent. People working in the East End told us that as we win people for Christ they leave for the suburbs. This was more true then than it is today, so the idea formed in my mind that someone ought to reverse the process and move in. And so without any clearly defined objective I did that when I was about 22.

Actual involvement in the community side came with David Sheppard who rang me up at the office one day to invite me to join a discussion group. He was running the Mayflower Family Centre in Canning Town. This discussion group was the start of the Urban Training Project.

Dowley is impressed by the radicalisation of the churches.

It isn't just political, but really a new Reformation, the church coming alive. The non-urban churches have changed their attitude: it's attributed to *Faith in the City* but that was more the evidence of an existing change. When you have a conversation now with suburban or non-urban Christians they ask the right questions instead of telling us the answers. That's a dramatic change. I don't distinguish between religious and the socio-political. Biblical faith is an indivisible religious and socio-political faith.

Today the idea of people like Jane Galbraith has caught on. It raises the problem whether outsiders can do the job. Theoretically no, but some gifted 'incomers' are better than some indigenous. In a run-down area you can't sever evangelism from social work.